# Let Me Call You Sweetheart: Trivia, legends, and lore about Valentine's Day

## An Outhouse Trivia Book

## By Christopher Forest

Dear readers,

Thanks so much for reading this edition of Outhouse Books. In *Let Me Call Your Sweetheart,* you will learn about the history of one of the most popular holidays – Valentine's Day. From facts about the saints known as Valentine, to superstitions, and little known folklore, this book will have you becoming a true Valentine.

Hopefully you enjoy this brand of specialized reader. It is designed for those of you who like to have a sense of accomplishment, but have limited time to read. These quick readers can be completed in one session....even in the privacy of your own "outhouse."

We hope you enjoy! Happy reading!!!

Sincerely,
The Outhouse Staff

# Outhouse Books

This book takes no responsibility for the claims made by way of the research conducted to complete it.

Outhouse Books also acknowledges all trademark rights to items mentioned in this text, including: Flowers.com™, Ask Men™, Hallmark™, NECCO™, Peanuts™, and Sweethearts™

Summary: A collection of interesting facts, trivia, and tidbits about Valentine's Day.

Author: Christopher Forest
Editor: Melissa Forest

ISBN:978-1482044508

Outhouse Books
Danvers, MA  01923
1 2 3 4 5 6 7 8 9 0 2
© 2013

# Valentine's Day of Yore

In the Middle Ages, young adults would celebrate the Valentine holiday by dipping their hands into a bowl of names as a way to pursue a loved one. Young men would choose the name of women and young women would choose the name of men.  They would then wear the name of the person pinned to their sleeve for an entire week. This was the origin of the phrase "wearing your heart on sleeve."

According to the traditions of the day, women in in the 1800s would often look for birds on Valentines Day. If a woman saw...

a sparrow, she would marry a poor person.
a robin, she would marry a sailor (or in later years, a police officer).
a crossbill, she would marry someone who would argue with her.
a blackbird, she would marry a minister.
a gold finch, she would marry a millionaire.
a bluebird, she would marry a happy person.
a dove, she would marry a faithful mate for life.
an owl, she would never marry.
and to not leave out our furry friends, if she saw a squirrel, she would marry a miser.

Thank Henry. King Henry VII of England officially decreed that February 14th be honored as St. Valentine's Day! Since then, the date has stuck.

Surprise! In England, it became a custom to leave gifts on the doorsteps of friends and loved ones the night before Valentine's Day. Often, the gifts were sent anonymously, with the message "Good-morrow to you Valentine."

Trick or Valentine. Centuries ago, children sometimes dressed up as adults on Valentine's Day. They would go door to door, knocking on neighbor's doors. When the door opened, the children would sing Valentine's Day songs.

That's one whale of a message! Sailors used to send their messages to loved ones by carving them in scrimshaw.

Spooning! The people of Wales have traditionally carved and given spoons as gifts on Valentine's Day. The gifts were symbolic of a tool used to unlock a person's heart. Thus, giving a spoon on Valentine's Day was the equivalent of giving a key to unlock a lover's heart.

Hidden messages. During the Victorian Era in England, boyfriends often hid messages or developed secret panels in cards they gave to their girlfriends. It was a way to prevent fathers – who often read any letters sent to their daughters – from learning how they truly felt about their beloved.

Valentine's Riddles  (answers follow on the next page).

1. What does a piano send his friends on Valentine's Day?

2. What does a male squirrel say to his girlfriend on Valentine's Day?

3. What do you call a person who falls head over heels in love on Valentine's Day?

4. What is Cupid's favorite school subject?

5. What did Ireland say to the ocean on Valentine's Day?

6. What does a sheep say to his wife on Valentine's Day?

Riddle answers

1. A Valentune

2. I am nuts about you

3. They've been Valen-swooned!

4. He-art

5. Isle be yours.

6. I love ewe.

# Valentine's Myths and Legends

According to legend, Cupid, the son of Venus, was said to shoot arrows at people to make them fall in love. Ignore those cartoons where lovers are shot in the posterior, because there is no truth to the rumor you had to be shot in the butt to fall in love. In fact, you had to be shot in the heart.

The original Valentine images of Cupid actually have him as a man. He ran around looking rather masculine, shooting arrows at people. During the 1800s, at the height of the renewed interest in Valentine's Day, the people in Victorian England felt uncomfortable with Cupid being depicted as a muscle man so he was transformed into a plump baby capable of shooting the love darts.

The English believed that the first person a woman saw on Valentine's Day was the person that she was going to marry. Hopefully, she liked what she saw.

Some people believe that St. Valentine's Day actually comes from the St. Galatin. He was a Norse saint whose named meant "lover of women." It is important to note that the letter G was pronounced like a V back in the days of Old Norse.

A rose is a rose? According to Roman mythology, the rose was the official flower of Venus. The flower was supposedly created by Cupid, who spilled nectar (one of the foods of the gods) on the ground. From this nectar, sprouted the first rose.

Ouch! Don't give a cactus as a gift on Valentine's Day. First, it may not be the best gift idea anyway. But, according to legend, it usually meant that a person was going to have an argument with the person he/she gave it to.

Perhaps, the argument actually stemmed from getting a cactus as a gift.

According to a Slovenia legend, St. Valentine brought the keys to "roots" for plants on Valentine's Day. Because of this, Valentine's Day is often the day that plants first start to bud and sprout.

On Valentine's Day, people used to purchase an apple and cut it open. They counted the number of seeds in the apple to predict how many children they would have.

Give me some glove! If you are single on Valentine's Day, and you find a missing glove outside, old superstition says you are in luck. Your future spouse will be found holding the other glove. Better hope he or she is not married.

In Lithuania and Latvia, particularly in the years following the end of the Soviet Union, it is customary for people to exchange and wear stickers on Valentine's Day.

It was once believed that if a girlfriend received an article of clothing from her boyfriend on Valentine's Day, she had to keep that article of clothing if she wanted to marry him.

Talk about a graveyard shift! In old England, sometimes, young women and older girls would go to a graveyard near a church at midnight. They would sing a love song while running around the church twelve times. And, if things went right, they would see a vision of their future husband.

Who knows what happened if things went wrong.

*Must see Valentine's movies.*

Want to see a good flick for Valentine's Day. Here's some that can't miss...for a variety of reasons (notes about each follow).

Gone With The Wind (1939)...long movie for historical buffs
Casablanca (1952)...classic romance
Sleeping Beauty (1959)...fairy tale love
Sleepless in Seattle (1993)...true love finds itself
Jerry Maguire (1996)...overcoming obstacles
Beauty and the Beast (2001)...great story and singing
The Notebook (2004)...how love overcomes all
Twilight (2008)...paranormal romance
Valentine's Day (2010)...what better for Valentine's Day
Date Night (2010)...good for a laugh

And for the family who might require something shorter, there is none better than the television special, *Be My Valentine, Charlie Brown.*

# Symbols of Valentines

Roses have long been given as a symbol of love. Ancient cultures, including the Greeks, used roses to represent the idea of love. And there is no more powerful way to show that love than to give a red rose.

In the 1980s, the diamond industry adopted Valentine's Day as their day. They suggested that it was the perfect time to send a "diamond" to the one you love.

You gotta have heart! The heart has long been associated with Valentine's Day because the heart is the traditional symbol of love. However, the idea of placing an arrow through the heart as a type of Valentine is also common. This symbolizes the inherent risk of sending someone a Valentine. There is always the possibility that he or she will not want to be the sender's Valentine.

The colors of Valentine's Day:

• red = symbol of love, strength, warmth, and feeling (it is also the color of the human heart)

• pink = innocence (and virginity)

• white = symbol of faith and purity, often associated with a pure love

What kind of heart is that? As anyone knows, the hearts given on Valentine's Day look nothing like a human heart. So where does the image come from. Well, according to urban legends and myths people believe the heart shape is connected to woman. It is often thought to be the image of a woman's lips pressed together, representing a kiss. Some people believe the image evolved from the shape of a woman's derriere. And, even some people claim the heart shape is associated with a woman with a well-endowed chest. Hmmmm.

Doves are often associated with Valentine's Day because of their partnerships. Since birds often chose their mates around Valentine's Day, this made sense. Likewise, both males and females help raise baby birds. And they both make a lovely cooing sound. Likewise, doves were often linked to magic and believed to bring good luck when seen (even if seen in dreams). The dove was also the bird that Noah saw as a promise from God that the flood would end. However, rather unluckily for the doves, the hearts of dead doves were often used in love potions.

Lovebirds are another bird often associated with Valentine's Day. These birds would often be imported from Africa. Sometimes, they did spread disease, so the importation of these birds was eventually made illegal.

Nothing beats chocolate. In Medieval days, woman would eat chocolate the night before Valentine's Day. They believed it would inspire dreams of future spouses.

Kisses are part of the art of Valentine's Day. However, watch which way you lean the next time you give your Valentine's Day kiss. You are twice as likely to lean to your right when you give that kiss than to your left.

Talk about romance. According to florists, the singularly most prefect flower to give on Valentine's Day, to express love, is a rose with baby's breath. Some florists call this the "signature rose."

At one time in Korea, it was custom to mourn Valentine's Day if one did not receive a gift. In fact, single people who did not receive a gift often gathered at restaurants and ate a dish made of black noodles.

Gloves are often considered a symbol of Valentine's Day. This dates back to England between the 17$^{th}$ and 19$^{th}$ century, where men often gave expensive gloves to their female loved ones on Valentine's Day.

What your flower says about your love...

According to the many flower websites, including *Pro Flowers.com,* the color of the flower you send can have an impact on the message that is sent.

Red flowers stand for love, overpowering feelings, and passion.

Pink flowers stand for grace and sophistication.

White flowers stand for pure love and faithfulness.

Orange flowers stand for desire and longing to be with someone.

Yellow flowers stand for true (or sometimes deep) friendship.

Purple flowers stand for magic and enchantment.

# Valentine's Cards

The earliest valentines were not cards or hearts. They were actually letters written and folded over, then sealed with wax. They were expensive to send at the time, and people had to find couriers willing to deliver the letters.

The first Valentine card sent to another person was delivered in 1415. It was written by the Duke of Orleans, a French aristocrat, who was captured by the British. A prisoner in the Tower of London, he longed to see his wife, Bonnie D'Armagnac, and sent her a love poem.  In it, he wrote, "I am already sick with love, my gentle Valentine." Sadly, though the Duke was released in 1440, he never saw his love again. She had died before he had returned. This original valentine is now located in the British Library in London.

The first modern Valentine style card was sent in 1824. From that time, "a Valentine" has been used as a term to denote such a card.

Thank Esther! Esther Howland is credited with making and sending the first popular Valentine cards in America. This entrepreneur from Massachusetts began mass-producing cards for the holiday in the 1840s. Her cards included lace and flowers. She was actually a student at Mount Holyoke College at the time she started her business (she had a little help from her father, who was a stationer). Howland became so good at it that she was known as the Mother of Valentine's Cards.

Penny Dreadfuls! This was the name of a popular Valentine card that appeared in the mid 1800s. Although they were cheap, the price matched the content of the card...they were often insulting and sent anonymously. They were sent because the price of postage went down at the time. Sometimes, they were even called Vinegar Valentines.

Calling all Juliets. Each year, the city of Verona, Italy becomes popular on Valentine's Day. According to sources, the city receives about 1000 Valentines each year addressed to its most legendary – albeit fictional character – Shakespeare's Juliet.

When you care enough to send the very best! Hallmark ™ has approximate 2000 cards designed for Valentine's Day.

Quiz time! Guess who receives the most Valentine's cards. You guessed it...teachers. Because giving Valentine's cards is a regular part of elementary school life, the most cards are given to teachers. Then comes children, mothers, and wives.

Kids between 6 and 10 are the biggest Valentine's Day card senders. More than 650 million cards are purchased for this age group (mainly for Valentine's parties at school).

Quotes for Valentine's Day

"All you need is love. But a little chocolate now and then doesn't hurt."
- Charles Schulz (*Peanuts* creator)

"I don't understand why Cupids was chosen to represent Valentine's Day. When I think about romance, the last thing on my mind is a short, chubby toddler coming at me a weapon."
-Author Unknown

"You know you're in love when you can't fall asleep because reality is finally better than your dreams.
-Dr. Seuss (children's author)

"Without Valentines day, February would be, well...January."
-Jim Gaffigan (comedian)

"A kiss is the shortest distance between two."
-Henny Youngman

# Valentine's Food

Want to send someone a "love apple?" All you'll need is a tomato. The term originated in the late 1570s, but no one is exactly sure how. It is believed that some people referred to tomatoes as Moorish apples.

Chocolate has long been associated with Valentine's Day. In the mid 1800s, doctors often prescribed chocolate to help soothe a broken heart. Richard Cadbury, of the Cadbury chocolate family fame, was the first person to capitalize on this idea. He convinced his father's company to create the first Valentine's chocolates.

The famous Sweethearts™ of Valentine's Day have been made since 1902 by the New England Confectionary Company. The candy maker, located in Massachusetts, has been making candies since 1847. They are famous for their well-known NECCO Wafers™. The company still has an original box of the wafers made more than a century ago. Incidentally, the candy was created by Daniel Chase, brother of NECCO™ founder Oliver Chase. He created the machine to stamp the wafers as well.

Sweetheart! The loveable sweetheart candies are actually prepared a year in advance. From February of the year before they are sold to the January of the year they *are* sold, the ever-loveable Valentine's candy is made consistently throughout the year. The total output of these hearts is about 100, 000 pounds per day. The reason – the candies typically sell out in about six weeks around Valentine's Day.

The first NECCO™ sweetheart shapes included more than just hearts. Horseshoes, baseballs, watches, and postcards rounded out the original score of sweethearts.

Eat to your sweethearts content! The NECCO™ sweetheart is a low calorie snack. Each wafer is about 6 calories.

Where do the sweethearts get all of those great sayings? Well, most of the sayings, such as *Kiss Me* and *Be Mine*, have existed since the candies were first made. However, each year, customers try to offer suggestions. Occasionally, NECCO™ tosses in new sayings, to stay hip to the times.

A love that lasts forever!! Want to impress you love with a special poem. You are not alone. Members of the first civilization, the Sumerians, actually did the same thing. The oldest love poem on record dates back to about 3500 BC and was written by a Sumerian.

Who's buying?  In Japan, it is customary for woman to give men a box of chocolates on Valentines Day (a practice started by clever marketing companies). But, to make for equal opportunity, men are expected to return the favor and give chocolate exactly one month later on March 14…known as White Day.

In the 1600s, people who lived in the cities of England gave food to friends and loved ones on Valentine's Day. The food given became so specific that the foods were often associated with the cities.

• In Peterborough England, plum buns (called Valentine's buns) were popular to give.

• In areas like Rutland, shuttle buns (shaped like a spinner's shuttle) were given.

• In Uppingham, gingerbread was the food of choice to give on Valentine's Day.

*Be My Valentine, Charlie Brown* quiz

Test your knowledge of this classic Charlie Brown special that premiered January 28, 1975. Check out the following page for the answers.

1. Why did Charlie Brown bring a suitcase with him for Valentine's Day?

2. Who does Linus purchase candy for?

3. Who has difficulty making a Valentine card?

4. What message does Charlie Brown receive on his candy heart?

5. Who feels so bad that she gives Charlie Brown a Valentine's card she received with her name crossed out?

6. Which Peanuts character, famous for always being a shepherd, went on hiatus for years after this episode (he did appear in the TV series in the 1980s and in later 1990s specials)?

*Be My Valentine, Charlie Brown* quiz answers.

1. He wanted to make sure he had enough room to carry all of his Valentines (he got none).

2. Miss Othmar, his teacher.

3. Sally (Snoopy shows her how to properly make one).

4. Forget it Kid!

5. Violet

6. Shermy

Following the original airing of *Be My Valentine, Charlie Brown*, kids across America felt so bad for Charlie Brown that they sent him Valentines.

# Valentine History

The word "Valentine" itself originally meant a sweetheart chosen on Valentine's Day. It believes to derive itself from the Latin word "Valentinus," two saints from Italy. The name Valentinus comes from the Latin word for strength.

Three different Saints are considered to be associated with St. Valentine's Day. All of these saints were martyred.

The most famous Saint that is honored by Valentine's Day is Valentinius, a Roman priest. The leaders of the Roman Empire imprisoned him in 269 AD for performing marriages for Roman soldiers – forbidden at the time. He was said to have healed the daughter of one of the jailers that imprisoned him, and may have fallen in love with her. According to legend, Valentinius even sent her a card that said "from you Valentine," right before he was executed…on February 14.

A second Valentine also lived in the Roman Empire. This Valentine, who was later sainted, was a bishop of Intermna (now the city of Terni in central Italy). In 197 AD, during the reign of Emperor Aurelius, he was one of the Christians persecuted and martyred during the empire's war against Christians.

Little is known about the third Valentine. A priest and missionary who went to Africa, he was later executed with fellow travelers. His head was preserved and in 1041 was put on display in the abbey of New Minster, Winchester in England.

In 496 AD, Pope Gelasius I declared the feast day of St. Valentine's to be February 14. This is not to be confused with the lover's holiday that is celebrated the same day (later established by the King of England). It was solely designed to commemorate the saint(s) known as Valentine. In 1969, the church removed the date from the calendar, claiming that there was no conclusive evidence to suggest who Valentine was or if he truly existed.

Approximating a date for Valentine's Day dates back to Old France. Using their old calendars, people who lived in France used to place the date of the first day of spring between February 7 and February 22 (the date often depended on the region and was based upon when birds chose mates). Love was often honored during this time of year.

In the 1300s, French and English courtiers developed the idea of choosing a sweetheart on Valentine's Day.

Some people associate the birth of Valentine's Day with the ancient Romans. On February 14th, the Romans celebrated the festival of Juno. The equivalent of the Greek's Hera, Juno was the queen of the gods and goddesses, and the goddess of marriage. Following that day, the festival of Lupercalia would begin, which paired up Roman girls and boys. The festival was known as the wolf festival and honored Romulus and Remus, who legendary founders of Rome.

According to Roman history, on Lupercalia was a time when the names of girls were put on slips of paper. The names of girls were placed in a jar; then boys would pull the names out. They would be partnered with the girl during the festival. Sometimes, the partnerships would last throughout the year and even lead to marriage.

Scary Valentines. During part of the Lupercalia celebration, men in ancient Rome would often run around with less clothing than usual as a way to celebrate the holiday.

Famed author Geoffrey Chaucer makes mention of Valentine's Day in the 1382, in the poem *Parliament of Fowls*. He mentions that "For this was Seynt Valentyne's Day. When every foul cometh ther to choose his mate."

The French sometimes claim to be the inventors of Valentine's Day. They believe it comes from the word "galantine" which means to be gallant or to be a lover.

Many Christian denominations shied away from recognizing Valentine's Day because of its association with the Roman pagan traditions. However, in the 1660s, the Church of England began to recognize it because of its popularity. In time, other churches followed.

Shakespeare makes mention of Valentine's Day in *Hamlet*. In the play, Ophelia says, "Good morrow! 'Tis Valentine's Day; All the morning betime; And I a maid at your window; To be your valentine!"

Most of the roses sent on Valentine's Day in the United States actually come from South America. In fact, more than 100 million total roses are sold and sent between February 12 and 14.

The Puritans of Boston brought the idea of Valentine's Day with them. Although it went contrary to the culture of the Puritans, many Puritans still celebrated covertly.

An orthodox Valentines? The Eastern Orthodox church still recognizes Valentine's Day as feast day. However, there are two separate holy days….in the summer! The Roman St. Valentine is honored on July 6th and the Bishop of Interamna (modern day Tierni) is honored on July 30.

Is it true?

Are the following statements about the human heart Fact or Fiction? Check out the answers on the following page.

1. The typical heart ways one pound.

2. The heart beats about 10,000 times a day.

3. Laughing can increase the blood flow through your heart.

4. The heart is electric.

5. It takes the heart about 1 minute to pump blood through the body.

Answers to heart quiz.

1. Fiction....it is more like 10 ounces.

2. Fiction....try more like 100,000 times a day

3. Fact...the effect may last up to 45 minutes

4. Fact...the electricity in the heart actually makes the muscle contract.

5. Fiction...it actually does the job in 20 seconds.

# Valentines By The Facts

XO. Ever wonder where the X came from as a symbol of a kiss. It dates back to medieval days. During that time period, many people could not read or write. In order to sign official documents, they would sign their name with a simple X. To show how important their "X" was, the writer would often kiss the mark before passing the paper to others. Hence, X not only marks the spot; it marks the kiss.

The best time to give a Valentine Day gift???
Men typically prefer to open their gifts in the
morning. However, women prefer to open
their gifts at night, preferably after dinner.

There are 150 million Valentine's Day cards exchanged on February 14. This makes it the second most popular card sending day each year. The first most popular is none other than Christmas.

In Finland, Valentine's Day is actually known as Friend's Day...a day to remember friends of all kinds.

Planning ahead. While most people think that guys come up with their Valentine's Day plans at the last minute, it turns out to be pure myth. Only 25 percent of men come up with a last second plan. Most guys actually have a well thought out Valentine's Day plan.

Happy chocolate day! More than 35 million boxes of chocolate are sold for Valentine's Day. Break out your candy now.

Date night. Men typically do a good job impressing their loved ones on Valentine's Day. It is one of the biggest date nights and the typical male spends about $130 on their date that night. Now that's a Valentine.

Men typically spend twice as much as women on Valentine's Day gifts and activities.

Although the Catholic Church has never been a proponent of Valentine's Day, nuns made some of the first official cards. These early cards often contained lace and flowers and pictures of Christian saints.

Save those hearts. The American Heart Association also celebrates Valentine's Day. Valentine's week is often known as "Save A Sweet Heart Week." It features the annual campaign to end smoking and therefore save more hearts.

It's a small world after all. Worldwide, more than 1 billion cards are sent on Valentine's Day.

Get those flowers early. The price of a dozen roses typically rises during the time around Valentine's Day – surprise, surprise. However, the price can jump nearly 30 percent.

The women have it. According to the Greeting Card Association, 85 percent of all Valentine's Cards are bought by women.

Happy Valen Woof's Day. About three percent of pet owners get Valentine's gifts for their pets. Now that is dedication.

Big bucks. Valentine's Day is one of the biggest buying days of the year. About $17.6 billion is spent on the holiday each year.

Oh, for me? About fifteen percent of women claim to send Valentine's flowers to themselves.

Between 26 million and 35 million heart shaped boxes of candy are purchased for Valentine's Day.

Valentine's Day is not just an American holiday. Many countries including, Australia, Canada, Denmark, England, France, Italy and Mexico get in the spirit of the day as well.

Sad, but true? According to some surveys, 4 in 10 people have a negative association with Valentine's Day.

The NO's have it. About 33 percent of men and 20 percent of women prefer to receive no gift on Valentine's Day.

The best way to their heart is through the stomach. Most women actually prefer a romantic dinner to a gift on Valentine's Day. So, guys, book that restaurant ASAP.

If you want to buy a gift...

According to the online magazine, *Ask Men*, if you want to earn big points with your significant other – and you're a guy – then the best way to do this with a gift is.

1. buy jewelry
2. buy couples dance lessons
3. buy a message gift certificate
4. buy a jewelry box

Almost half of all Valentine's cards are purchased less than a week before the holiday.

According to the U.S. Census, 65% of adult Americans celebrate Valentine's Day with a card. About 44 percent of Americans have a date night. And more people exchange candy (38 percent of Americans) than flowers (32 percent). The other gift ideas are purchasing gift cards, getting a plush doll, buying perfume or cologne, and buying jewelry.

How many words can you make using the word Valentine.

Example: Teal

# It Happened on Valentine's Day

Alexander Graham Bell applied for the patent for his telephone on Valentines Day, 1876. He called his invention an "Improvement in Telegraphy." Incidentally, he had originally developed the device to help people who are deaf hear and communicate.

Welcome to America. In 1912, Arizona was officially admitted to the Union, becoming the 48<sup>th</sup> state.

Celebrate a birthday on Valentine's Day. You are in good company. Here are ten other people with Valentine's birthdays...

Jack Benny – comedian – born in 1894
Drew Bledsoe – NFL quarterback – born 1972
Michael Bloomberg – mayor of New York – 1942
Hugh Downs – TV journalist – 1921
Florence Henderson – Actor, *Brady Bunch*™ mom – 1934
Jimmy Hoffa – union leader – 1913
Jim Kelly – football quarterback – 1960
Victor Morrow – TV and movie actor – 1929
Christopher Sholes – inventor of the typewriter – 1819
Teller – the quiet magician of Penn and Teller fame – 1948

Get out the Vote! In 1920, the League of Women Voters was founded by Carrie Chapman Catt in Chicago. It helped spearhead efforts to gain women's right to vote that year.

In 1929, Sir Alexander Fleming was able to help save the world by introducing them to a modern medicine. It was on this day that penicillin was introduced to the world. Fleming made the discovery by accident when he left a plate of staphylococcus bacteria uncovered. Mold fell into the plate and Fleming noticed that many of the bacteria had been killed.

Alexander's events of 1929 would probably have more acclaim had they not been overshadowed by the events of that occurred in Chicago. On this day, members of Al Capone's gang ordered a kill on members of George "Bugs" Moran's gang. Seven members of his gang were killed in the *St. Valentine's Day Massacre*.

In 1939, the German government under Adolph Hitler launched the *Bismarck*. It was the largest battleship of the time and became of the scourge of the North Atlantic. The British navy took great lengths to destroy the ship, particularly after it sunk the HMS Hood in May 1941. The British hunted the ship until sinking it in September, 1941.

Now that's a house. In 1962, Jacqueline Kennedy gave a famous televised tour of the White House. The tour was so popular that it is believed 75 percent of Americans watched it.

What a day to be married:
Here are some famous couples married on
Valentine's Day...

Captain and Tennille
Jerry Garcia and Deborah Koons
Meg Ryan and Dennis Quaid
Pamela Anderson and Tommy Lee

# Valentine unscramble

Use the clues to find the answer. Then, use the letters at the beginning of each word to unscramble a hidden message related to Valentine's Day. Answers are on the following page.

1. These are the all important three words for Valentine's Day. ____    ____ ____ ____ ____

____ ____ ____

2. Venus was in love with this Roman god of war.

____ ____ ____ ____

3. The famous Howland that popularized the Valentine's Day card.

_____ _____ _____ _____ _____ _____

4. Woman would often look to this animal to predict what type of husband they would have.

____ ____ ____ ____ ____

5. The Greek god of love:    _____ ____ ____ ____

6. This is the company that has perfected the sweethearts candy heart. ____ ____ ____ ____ ____ ™

Answers to Valentine's quiz.

1. I love you
2. Mars
3. Esther
4. Birds
5. Eros
6. NECCO™

Letters to unscramble I M E B E N

Unscrambles to form BE MINE

If you were born on February 14

Your sign of the zodiac: Aquarius

Qualities: passionate, creative, energetic, worrier

Career: Typically, they tend to pursue careers that will allow them to enjoy free time as well.

You are known for being energetic, passionate, and cheerful. You are inventive and clever; and would have the penchant for making a good business leader. You do tend to be a worrier at times, which can get the best of you. You do love the spotlight and can be passionate when falling in love.

Resources

Austin, K. Jessie. "Little Known Facts About Valentine's Day. *Yahoo.com*. URL: http://voices.yahoo.com/little-known-facts-valentines-day-786223.html

Born on February 14th". *Nndb.com.* URL: http://www.nndb.com/lists/562/000106244/

Chen, Will. "Weird Thirds Your Didn't Know About Valentine's Day. *Wisebread.com.* URL: http://www.wisebread.com/weird-things-you-didnt-know-about-valentines-day

"Eighteen Financial Facts About Valentine's Day." *MSNBC.com.* URL: http://money.msn.com/saving-money-tips/post.aspx?post=2b3c62b2-7941-4ca4-853b-4cbc7250913f

"Facts About Love." *She.knows.com.* URL: http://www.sheknows.com/holidays-and-seasons/articles/807655/fun-facts-about-valentine-s-day

"February 14th Birthday Astrology." *TLC.com.* URL: http://tlc.howstuffworks.com/family/february-14-birthday-astrology.htm

"February 14th horoscope." *Café Astrology.com.* URL http://www.cafeastrology.com/birthday/february14_2012.html

"History of Valentine's Day." *Morristown.com.* URL: http://www.morristown.com/Valentines Day/ValentinesDay.html

Kids Valentine Trivia Part I. *Kids Turn Central.* URL: http://www.kidsturncentral.com/games/trivia/vtrivia.htm

Lorenzi, Rosella, "The Seedy, Scandalous History of Valentine's Day." *Discovery News*. URL:
http://news.discovery.com/history/history-valentines-day-121302.html

"The Origins of Valentine's Day." *Learnenglish.de*. URL:
http://www.learnenglish.de/culture/ValentinesDay.htm

Rando, Anthony. "Five Morsels of Valentine's Trivia. *Easton Patch*. URL:
http://easton.patch.com/articles/five-morsels-of-valentine-s-trivia

Shallcross, Aida. "Ten Facts About Sweethearts Candies." *Yahoo.com*. URL:
http://voices.yahoo.com/10-facts-sweethearts-candies-5319711.html?cat=22

"Six Little Known Facts About Valentine's Kisses." *The fun times guide.* URL:
http://holidays.thefuntimesguide.com/2007/02/facts_about_kisses.php

"St. Valentine's Day Superstitions." *Superstitionsof.com.* URL: http://www.superstitionsof.com/st-valentines-day-superstitions.htm


"St. Valentine's Day Trivia." *Fun Trivia.com.* URL: http://www.funtrivia.com/en/subtopics/St-Valentines-Day-Trivia-165669.html


"Valentine." *Online Etymology Dictionary*. URL: http://www.etymonline.com/index.php?term=valentine


"Valentine's Day Facts." *Mydearvalentine.com.* URL: http://www.mydearvalentine.com/valentines-day-facts/


"Valentine's Day History Legends and Supersititions." *Supersititionsonline.com*. URL: http://superstitionsonline.com/valentines-day/

"Valentines Day History, Symbols, Folklore, and Phobias. *Brownie Locks.com*. URL: http://www.brownielocks.com/valentine history.html

"What Are Some Well Known Valentine's Trivia Facts. *Askville.com.* URL: http://askville.amazon.com/Valentine%27s-Day-trivia-facts/AnswerViewer.do?requestId=3974 1346

"What Happened on February 14th: This Day in History." *The People's History.com.* URL: http://www.thepeoplehistory.com/february14th.html

Thank you so much for reading our book. Please check out other Outhouse trivia titles as well. If you do have any questions or comments, or feedback about the trivia, don't hesitate to contact us at Outback Books.

WE WISH YOU – ALWAYS – A HAPPY VALENTINE'S DAY!

www.ingramcontent.com/pod-product-compliance
Lightning Source LLC
Chambersburg PA
CBHW070705290526
45790CB00001B/451